Burden

Burden

Postcards from the
Collection of John Kasmin

Burden

Trivia Press

Postcards and Burden

In the heyday of the postcard, the first decades of the 20th century, photographers roamed the streets and byways of the world seeking subjects that would provide interesting pictures for people to send in the mail as adornments to their mainly banal messages. Among the scenes of life that attracted them were the ubiquitous bearer of things – the porters and shoppers, the perambulating traders, the women laden with firewood, water and offspring – and all those who could not afford a donkey or other working beast.

For many years I have sought out and bought cards showing the variety and awful hardship this carrying revealed. Women seem to have had the worst of it before the internal combustion engine and the fork-lift truck arrived. Indeed, even today we see our wives weighed down with shopping bags and schoolchildren bent beneath backpacks of text books, but the splendidly diverse burdens displayed in this book are now only found in remote mountain kingdoms and the roadless regions of the world.

TIBETIAN OLD WOMAN COOLIE   S. SINGH

POLESIE. Poleszuk z siecią

Constantinople. Marchand de charbon.

Le Caire, Marchand de poissons.

Nr. 116. Au Carto-Sport, Max H. Rudmann, Le Caire.

SANDWICH MAN

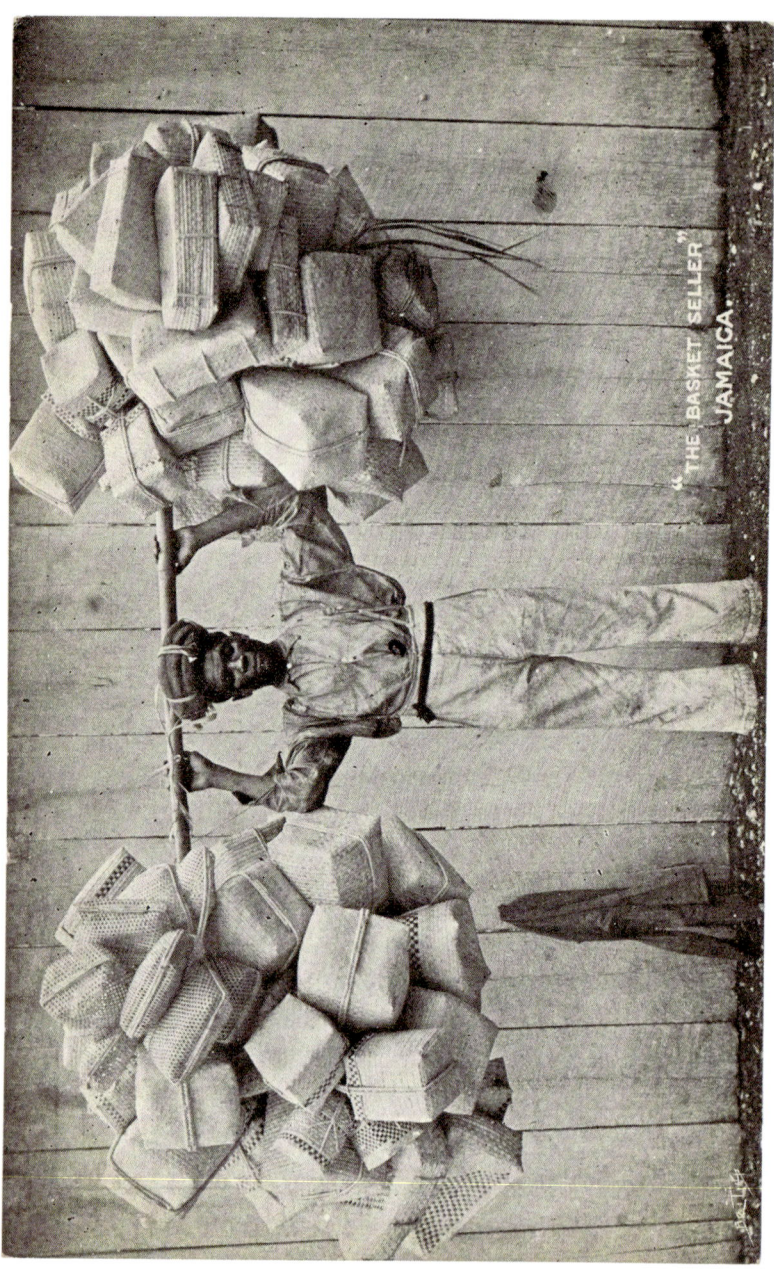
"THE BASKET SELLER" JAMAICA.

Tananarive. - Marchand de Poterie.

Mexico. Vendedor de tablas.

LE CANTAL PITTORESQUE
62 - Sur la Montagne — Le montage du Parc

Indio. Niño de Kamac, llevando 125 libras hoja de caña de Azucar.
Boy carrying 125 lbs. sugar cane leaves.

587 "A Lakeland Dalesman"
(Abraham's Series)

Chinoise se rendant en visite.

Vlaardingsche Koffiejongen.

Dahomey — Ouidah, Porteuses de sable.

Comerciantes indígenas. Camino Chichicastenango.

Heimkehr von der Krokodiljagd

323. Tonkin - Mans en Route

TONKIN — Hanoï — Femmes employées à la manufature de Tabac

Costume del Lazio - Venditrice di castagne

2408 Alterocca Terni

Phot-Edit. O. Lefevre, Calais

309. *Voulez-Vous d'Zallumettes!* — 1908
Bien connue des Calaisiens et des campagnes environnantes, cette intrépide marchande guinoise exerce son métier depuis plus de 50 ans, faisant le trajet à pied, avec ses bagages, de Guines à Calais, et *vice versa*, plusieurs fois par semaine.

10513-39   LONDON LIFE. A SWEEP   ROTARY PHOTO, E.C

Bengali bread seller, Singapore.

Piboule et Rouzinier: Types Châtelleraudais
Ch. Arambourou - phot., Châtellerault.

SOMALIA ITALIANA: DIAVOLETTO SOMALO

Just geting home from the Post Office - with 92 lbs of Mail that had accumulated during the winter there was that much for me - and some even had more so you see we have our inconveniencys up here it lays in Seattle untill spring - and at the opening of Navigation the forward it -

J. J. 8209 Fromagers Suisses

Jullien frères, Phot. Editeurs, Genève

Marchande de poules

"LUMPS OF COAL."
(COAL WOMAN OF ST. THOMAS, D.W.I.)

Les p'tits métiers de Paris
J'ai du bon mouron pour les p'tits oiseaux....

MISSIONS des P. P. du SAINT-ESPRIT — La corvée de bois

Portefaix arabe

Chinese beggar carrying her babies.

Типы Россіи.—Types de Russie. № 49.
Торговка чулками.—Marchande de bas.

carregando um piano.

NÉRIS-LES-BAINS (Allier)
67 — Les lavandières revenant du ruisseau de Courneauron

Albert M. Editeur

BLANCHISSEUSE LIMOUSINE.

194. - Les Schlitteurs gravissant la Montagne et portant leurs Schlittes - Forêt de l'Urson

LES VOSGES PITTORESQUES

Photo Homeyer et Ehret, Epinal

Territoire de Kouang-Tchéou-Wan. — Groupe de Cultivateurs.

Shanghai. - Carrying Josh papers.

732 ANICHE — La Verrerie — Les Porteuses de Canons J.D.V.

KHASIAS CARRYING THAPA.

Compañia Huanchaca de Bolivia

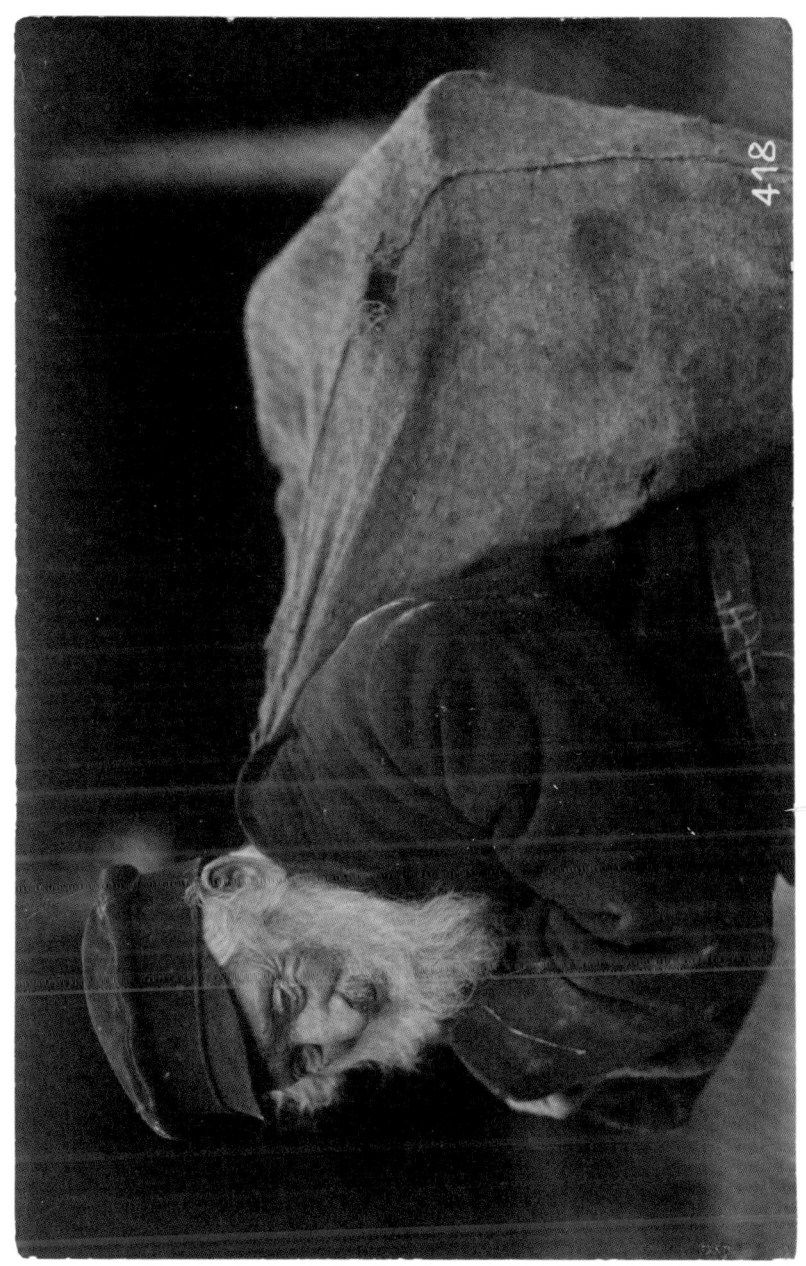

Cafétier ambulant. Souvenir de Constantinople 10/9 903

Photogr. Sébah & Joaillier.

Marchand d'habits

VIVIER-AU-COURT. — Madame Dominé, Appariteur
partant de la mairie pour coller des affiches, âgée de 85 ans toujours vive
et alerte, appariteur de la commune depuis de longues années
est sans doute la doyenne des appariteurs de France

WOMAN AND CHILD.
Series 50—By Reef and Palm. Kerry (Copyright) Sydney.

Русскiе типы - Types russes
Чемоданщикъ - Merchand de malles.

Native Milk Carrier, S.A.

274. Angola — Tocadores

Mar 16/05

Dear Dorothy / Do you think you could play this instrument?

Osorio & Seabra — Loanda — Editores

11804 - Paysannes du Valais   Walliser Bäuerinnen

Jüdischer Scherenschleifer

1398. - Nos Vieux professionnels bretons
Un bûcheron de la forêt du Huelgoat

Editorial Note

Country of origin: *the country in which the postcard was produced, rather than the country in which the photograph was taken.*

Real photograph: *the postcard was developed onto photographic paper, rather than being a gravure reproduction.*

Published: *multiple copies of the postcard were published, showing that it was intended for public rather than private use.*

Unused: *the postcard has never been written on or posted.*

Notes on the Postcards

6 Germany
Published. Unused.
c.1903

7 India
Real photograph.
Unused

8 Poland
Real photograph.
Unused

9 Turkey
Published.
Unused

10 France
Published.
Used 1907

This is heavy rye bread. The photo has been retouched with outlines on her figure.

Let us hope this chest is empty and photographer Singh of Darjeeling has posed it for us.

This contraption serves to trap water birds in the Pripet Marshes.

Delivering coal in Istanbul.

Selling statuary in the streets of Bordeaux.

11 Egypt
Published.
Unused

12 UK
Published.
Unused

13 Switzerland
Published.
Used 1903

A walking fish shop in Cairo.

A moving advertisement in Oxford Street, London.

Once one would have hired a commissionaire like this man in Geneva to lug home one's shopping for a fee.

14 UK
Published. 1909

15 France
Published. Used 1908

A basket pedlar in Jamaica. I like the tall fence of wide planks and his jacket hanging on it. He wears braces and a belt of sorts – his pads almost Rastafarian.

A pot vendor in Madagascar, barefoot in a marketplace.

16 USA
Real photograph.
Published. c.1920

Two lads in overalls coming from the river, each carrying two pails braced apart, covered and containing we know not what that must not be spilt.

17 France
Published.
Unused

A scene in Natitingou in the north of Dahomey, now Benin. Somba men wearing only their penis sheaths, and the odd bangle as necklace, although the youngest has lost his or doesn't warrant one yet. Oil drums cut in half to carry their loads.

18 Mexico
Published.
Unused. c.1902

A plank salesman.

19 France
Published.
Used 1912

A farm labourer carries a section of wooden fence that will form part of a holding pen for beasts – in the Cantal region of France.

20 Switzerland
Real photograph.
Unused

The old Swiss way of transporting salt blocks.

21 Guatemala
Published.
Unused

He is bearing 125 pounds of sugar cane leaves.

22 UK
Real photograph.
Published.
Unused

Collecting a lost sheep in the Lake District.

23 Germany
Published.
Used 1903

Rather unconvincing hunting trophies for sale.

24 South Africa
Real photograph.
Used 1939

She appears to be moving house.

"THE BASKET SELLER"
JAMAICA.

25 Ethiopia
Real photograph.
Unused. 1930s

The loveliest porter.

26 France
Published.
Unused

Taking his wife on a visit – a Chinese form of courtesy.

27 Holland
Published.
Used 1905

A lad who delivers coffee-cans to workers and perhaps there are cakes in the three bags.

28 USA
Real photograph.
Unused

Ceramic basins of unknown purpose but prone to accident.

29 USA
Real photograph.
Unused

Overladen with untidy and unlabelled packages in New York. And they can't be hats.

30 India
Real photograph.
Unused

Bhutanese tribal people selling milk they carry in these beautiful wooden cylinders.

31 Unknown
Real photograph.
Unused

A Central European housewife – perhaps going to feed her pigs? Such a fine photograph surely needs no explanation.

32 France
Published.
Unused. c.1930

A file of handsome young women with panniers of millet on their heads enter an African village.

33 France
Published.
Unused

Women in Dahomey transporting sand for building works. They rest with the white sand in bowls on their heads and their foreman stands among them. Ouidah, or Whydah, was the place Bruce Chatwin's 'Viceroy' used as his home base when gathering slaves for export to Brazil in the early 19th century – I visited it with him in 1978.

34 Guatemala
Real photograph.
Used 1935

Indian pedlars shifting their stock of chairs and pots.